PLAY SHOWTIME

Hits from the Greatest Shows of All Time

BOOK I

Solos for violin with piano accompaniment
arranged by Fred Glover and Roy Stratford

Contents

© 1989 by Faber Music Ltd
First published in 1989 by Faber Music Ltd
3 Queen Square London WC1N 3AU
Music drawn by New Notations
Cover design and typography by Studio Gerrard
Printed in England by Halstan & Co Ltd
All rights reserved

ISBN 0 571 51588 6

FABER *ff* MUSIC

What Kind Of Fool Am I?

(Stop The World – I Want To Get Off)

Music and original lyrics by
Leslie Bricusse and Anthony Newley

Ped.

Memory
(Cats)

Music by Andrew Lloyd Webber
Original lyrics by Trevor Nunn
after T.S. Eliot

Waltz – Love Unspoken
(*The Merry Widow*)

Music by Franz Lehár
Original lyrics by Viktor Leon and Leo Stein

Arrangement © 1989 Glocken Verlag Ltd
for the British Commonwealth of Nations, its protectorates,
dependencies and mandated territories, Eire and the United States of America
Original publisher Ludwig Doblinger (Bernard Herzmansky), Vienna.

Younger Than Springtime
(*South Pacific*)

Music by Richard Rodgers
Original lyrics by Oscar Hammerstein II

9

I Don't Know How To Love Him

(*Jesus Christ Superstar*)

Music by Andrew Lloyd Webber
Original lyrics by Tim Rice

Maria
(West Side Story)

Music by Leonard Bernstein
Original lyrics by Stephen Sondheim

The Music Of The Night
(*The Phantom Of The Opera*)

Music by Andrew Lloyd Webber
Original lyrics by Charles Hart & Richard Stilgoe

16

Hey There!
(The Pajama Game)

Music and original lyrics by
Richard Adler and Jerry Ross

I Could Have Danced All Night

(*My Fair Lady*)

Music by Frederick Loewe
Original lyrics by Alan Jay Lerner

On My Own
(*Les Misérables*)

Music by Claude-Michel Schönberg
Original lyrics by Alain Boublil, Herbert Kretzmer,
John Caird, Trevor Nunn & Jean-Marc Natel